Everything You Need To Know About

ALCOHOL

Teens often feel pressured to drink with friends.

• THE NEED TO KNOW LIBRARY •

Everything You Need To Know About

ALCOHOL

Barbara Taylor

Series Editor: Evan Stark, Ph.D.

THE ROSEN PUBLISHING GROUP, INC.
NEW YORK

Published in 1989 by The Rosen Publishing Group, Inc.
29 East 21st Street, New York City, New York 10010

First Edition
Copyright 1989 by The Rosen Publishing Group, Inc.

Manufactured in the United States of America.

Library of Congress Cataloging-in-Publication Data

Taylor, Barbara, 1938–
    Everything you need to know about alcohol / Barbara Taylor—1st
ed.
    (The Need to know library)
    Bibliography: p. 62
    Includes index.
    Summary: Describes the effect of alcohol on mind and body
and directs those in jeopardy where to seek help.
    ISBN 0-8239-0813-5 :
    1. Alcoholism—Juvenile literature. 2. Alcohol—Physiological
effect—Juvenile literature. [1. Alcoholism] I. Title.
II. Title: Alcohol. III. Series
RC565.T38 1988
613.8′1—dc19   88-39820
                                                                          CIP
                                                                           AC

Contents

Introduction

This book is about alcohol use and abuse. It is about drinking alcohol. It is about some of the things that can happen to people who drink alcohol.

A person who drinks can become an alcoholic. An alcoholic has *alcoholism*. That is the disease that some people get because of drinking. An alcoholic is addicted to alcohol—just as a heroin addict is addicted to heroin.

It usually takes a long time for a person who drinks to become alcoholic. So you may think that young people cannot become alcoholics. That is not true. If you start to drink when you are very young, you can become dependent on alcohol. You need not drink every day. You need not get drunk often. But you can become an alcoholic by the time you are a teenager.

Some people can drink every day without becoming alcoholic. Some people can get drunk more than once in a while and not become alcoholic. But when you drink alcohol you can have other serious problems.

Alcohol can be deadly. Alcoholism can cause death in extreme cases. But there is another way, too, that alcohol can cause death. Drinking and driving is called DWI—driving while intoxicated. It is the cause of a large percentage of automobile accidents. These accidents can happen in small towns or on main streets. They can happen on farm lanes, or on highways, or freeways. Not every drunk driver is a teenager, but many are. Drunk drivers can kill others along with themselves. Or they can kill others and live. Then they have to pay the price. Even if they are not sent to prison, they have to suffer a lifetime of guilt.

Alcohol use and alcoholism are serious matters. Your friends may offer you alcoholic drinks. You may be afraid they won't like you if you say no. But remember one important thing. No one will ever care as much about you as you do about yourself. You must make your own decisions. You must control your own life.

Use this book to help you decide. When you have all the facts, you can make the right choice on your own.

There are many kinds of alcohol for a variety of uses.

Chapter 1

What Is Alcohol?

There are many kinds of alcohol. Most of them are deadly poison to drink.

Amyl alcohol and *propyl alcohol* are used to dissolve things like paint and tar.

Butyl alcohol is sometimes called butanol. It is used in insect sprays and in the paint used on highways.

Methyl alcohol is also called wood alcohol. It is used in cleaning solutions, paint removers, and antifreeze. Antifreeze keeps the water in a car radiator from freezing. Methyl alcohol is also used in shaving lotions, hair sprays, and rubbing alcohol. Rubbing alcohol is put on the skin to soothe muscles and to lower high fever.

Denatured alcohol is ethyl alcohol with poisons added. It is used in paints and dyes and for cleaning the skin.

The beverage alcohol is *ethyl alcohol*. This is the alcohol we will be talking about.

Making Alcohol

Ethyl alcohol is made by *fermentation*. In this process the starch and sugar in natural products such as potatoes, fruits (grapes, apples, plums), and grains (barley, rye, corn, wheat) are changed into ethyl alcohol.

You may have seen the result of fermentation. Did you ever leave milk out of the refrigerator overnight in a warm room? Fermentation caused the milk to smell and taste different.

Yeast causes these changes. Yeast plants travel in the air. They are so tiny that they are invisible to the naked eye. They land on the warm milk.

Beer

The process of making beer is called *brewing*. In brewing, a liquid mixture of yeast is added to a mixture of malted cereals (barley, rye, corn, wheat, and others). The yeast *ferments* the grain, changing it to alcohol. When fermentation stops, the liquid is beer. Tiny dried flower buds called hops are added to the liquid for flavor. Hops also help preserve the beer.

Ale is made from the same ingredients as beer. The alcoholic content of ale is slightly higher.

Light beer has fewer calories and a lower alcoholic content than regular beer.

THINGS TO FERMENT TO GET ALCOHOLIC DRINKS

Grains

Grapes

Apples

Cherries

Potatoes

Plums

Dark beer (stout, bock beer, porter) is named for its darker color. Dark beers contain more alcohol than most other beers. The taste of dark beer is stronger and sweeter.

Three point two beer (sometimes called three-two beer) contains no more than 3.2 percent alcohol. In some areas people can buy 3.2 beer at a younger age than the legal age for buying regular beer.

Near beer is fermented like regular beer, but most of the alcohol is taken out.

Wine

Wine is also made by natural fermentation. Most wine is made from grapes. But some wine is made from other fruits and even from vegetables.

Wine makers add yeast to warm fruit or vegetable juice. The yeast changes the sugar in the juice. The change produces alcohol and a gas called *carbon dioxide*. The gas is allowed to escape. The

11

juice sits and ferments. When fermentation stops, the juice is wine.

Wines can be white, red, or rosé, depending on the kind of grape that is used. Wine is *sweet* or *dry*. A wine can be sweetened with unfermented sugar. Dry wines contain only a small amount of sugar. Wines can be *carbonated*. These are called *sparkling wines*. Champagne is a sparkling wine. Carbon dioxide is added after fermentation to give the wine its bubbles. Madeira, port, and sherry are *fortified wines*. They contain more alcohol than other wines.

Liquor

Whiskey, rum, vodka, gin, brandy, and stronger alcoholic beverages are made by *distillation*. The fermented liquid is heated in a machine called a

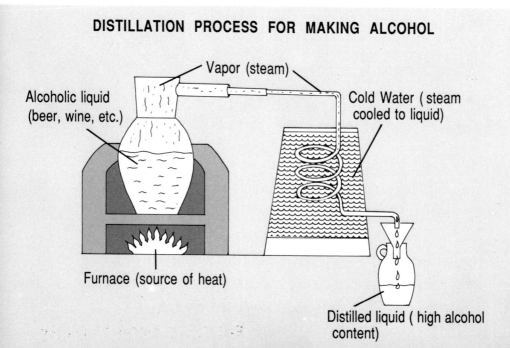

DISTILLATION PROCESS FOR MAKING ALCOHOL

Vapor (steam)

Alcoholic liquid (beer, wine, etc.)

Cold Water (steam cooled to liquid)

Furnace (source of heat)

Distilled liquid (high alcohol content)

still. The industrial plant where liquor is made is
called a *distillery*.

In distillation, a fermented liquid that contains
alcohol is heated. The alcohol in the wine or beer
vaporizes. That means it becomes steam. The steam
is collected and cooled. As the steam cools, it
becomes a liquid that is nearly pure alcohol.
Flavorings and water are added to this alcohol.

Some of the popular distilled beverages are:

○ **Whiskey** (rye, scotch, bourbon): made by
   distilling the fermented juice of cereal grains
   such as rye, corn, or barley.
○ **Gin:** made by distilling rye and other grains and
   flavoring the alcohol with juniper berries.
○ **Vodka:** distilled from rye malt, fermented
   potatoes, or fruit such as apples.
○ **Rum:** made from fermented molasses or the
   juice of sugarcane.
○ **Brandy:** distilled from wine. It can be made
   from grapes and other fruits such as plums,
   apples, cherries, and apricots.
○ **Liqueurs:** distilled beverages made by adding
   fruit and herbs to brandy. People usually drink
   them after dinner.

Alcohol as a Food

All alcohol, fermented or distilled, is a food.
That means that the body oxidizes it—unites it
with oxygen. This process produces energy, so

alcohol provides the body with calories. One ounce of alcohol has about 160 calories.

Providing fattening calories is all that alcohol does for the body. Alcohol contains no nutrients, vitamins, or minerals.

Alcohol as a Drug

When people hear the word "drug," they usually think of illegal street drugs such as marijuana, heroin, or cocaine. Sometimes they think of prescription medicines—the drugs doctors prescribe to help patients get well. People seldom think of alcohol when they hear the word "drug." But alcohol *is* a drug—the most widely used drug in the world.

Like all drugs, alcohol causes changes in the human body. Alcohol acts as a depressant on the body's nervous system. A depressant slows a person down.

Watch a person who has had quite a bit to drink in a short time. You will see the depressant at work. You will notice the drinker's speech becoming slurred. You will see that his or her steps become staggered. Toss a ball toward the drinker. He or she will probably have trouble catching it. A person's reflexes become dulled when the nervous system slows down.

After a few drinks, even simple tasks can become difficult.

Why Is Alcohol Legal?

Most drugs are not legal. To buy them, people need permission from a doctor. But it is legal to buy and to drink alcohol.

Alcohol is different from other drugs such as heroin and cocaine. A person normally does not "need" another drink. Alcohol does not cause addiction (physical need for a drug) or dependency (strong desire to take a drug often) except in people who are *alcoholics*. An alcoholic is a person who has the disease called *alcoholism*. Alcoholics cannot control their need for alcohol. And when they drink, they cannot stop.

Some people think alcohol should not be legal. They point to the millions of alcoholics and the

15

great number of deaths caused by drinking and driving. In 1919 Congress passed the 18th Amendment to the Constitution. It was called the Prohibition Amendment. It forbade the making and sale of alcohol. In 1933 the law was changed again. People decided they wanted to have the choice. Congress passed another amendment to the Constitution, which was called the Repeal Amendment.

Fact Sheet

○ **100 million Americans drink alcohol.** Eight out of ten men over age 21 and six out of ten women over age 21 drink alcoholic beverages, at least occasionally.

○ **Alcohol kills.** Alcohol is a factor in nearly half of the suicides, murders, and accidental deaths in the U.S. Alcohol claims at least 100,000 lives each year, 25 times as many as all illegal drugs combined.

○ **Alcohol causes problems on U.S. roads.** Each year there are nearly 50,000 deaths on U.S. highways, and alcohol use by drivers is responsible for half of those deaths, especially on weekends.

○ **Alcohol hurts young people.** Five thousand teenagers are killed and 130,000 are injured each year in drunken driving accidents.

Chapter 2

Attitudes Toward Alcohol

Alcohol use by adults is legal almost everywhere in the United States. But many people have mixed feelings about alcohol.

For some people the words "alcohol," "drink," or "drinker" bring negative feelings. These words make some people think of the problems alcohol use can cause.

Some people have little understanding about the use of alcohol. Some nondrinkers do not understand people who drink. Some drinkers do not trust people who do not drink.

Negative feelings can be harmful. They can prevent people from talking about subjects that are important to them.

Experts say it is important for young people to talk about alcohol with adults they respect. The experts say that people should have a chance to express their opinions. They need to talk about the use of alcohol and how to control it.

Young people should be sure of where they stand on the subject of alcohol. Otherwise they can be talked into drinking when they really do not want to drink.

The Story of Maria

"I could die!" Ginny squealed when her best friend told her the news. Ginny grabbed Maria's hands and they spun round and round like teammates who had just won the championship.

"Tell me again!" Ginny yelled. "He actually *asked* you to go with him to the class picnic?"

Maria admitted it was amazing. Greg was the undisputed king of the school.

Maria lived on Cloud Nine for the next two weeks. She got a loan from her mother to buy a new sweater. She huddled with her friends and told them over and over how Greg had asked her out.

Maria was ready a full hour before Greg was due to arrive. She liked what she saw in the mirror. To her relief, she was looking well again. Over the last couple of months the strain of her grandfather's illness had affected her. The whole family was

It's all right to refuse a drink.

upset. Maria was thankful that the date with Greg had taken her mind off her grandfather.

The picnic was all that Maria had expected. Everyone was having fun. Greg showed her a great deal of attention. He seemed quieter, though, than Maria had expected.

The band finished setting up for the evening of dancing. Greg leaned toward Maria and whispered, "Let's go. This is a drag. I know where there's a great party."

When they arrived, Maria was surprised. Most of the people were older, and there was a lot of noise. Greg seemed to know everyone. Someone handed him two paper cups, one for him and one for Maria.

"Drink up," Greg said to Maria. "We're going to have fun."

Everyone was still watching as Maria brought the cup to her lips. The smell from the cup hit her. It was just like the smell in Grandpa's room. Maria hated it. She shoved the cup toward Greg. He grabbed it and gulped it down. Everyone cheered. "Come on, Maria," he said, "get with it. Bottoms up."

"Take me home," Maria whispered to Greg. Greg laughed, then walked away. Maria went home from the party by herself.

Months later, Maria's mother told her about meeting Greg's mother. Greg was in the hospital, she said—the same hospital Grandpa had been in. Greg was getting the same kind of treatment that Grandpa had received—treatment for alcoholism.

Understanding Your Values

Teenagers receive many messages about alcohol. Some of the messages about alcohol are direct.

Some of the messages are beer commercials. Between the ages of two and eighteen, children in the United States see 100,000 beer commercials. Most of these commercials try to show that drinking beer makes life more fun.

Drinking alcohol can cause depression.

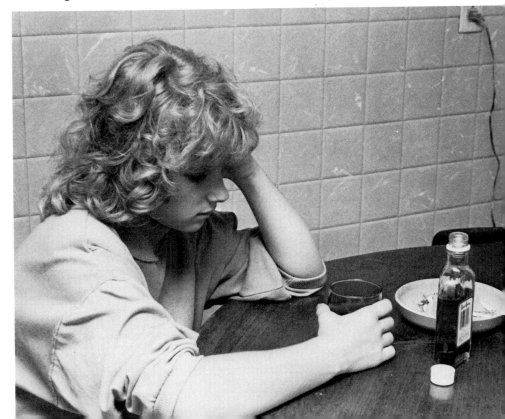

Some messages about alcohol come to teenagers indirectly. For example, teens may see an adult get behind the wheel of a car after drinking a lot at a party. Or they may see an adult who has been drinking a lot embarrass a friend. Young people might think this is okay.

Actually, neither behavior is acceptable. Alcohol is never an excuse for bad judgment or rude behavior.

As a teenager, you should be aware of your values. You should think about them, make decisions about what you believe and how you feel, and then remember those values when the time comes to decide about your own behavior.

What Would I Do?

Here are two stories. Read each one. Then choose the ending you think best describes what the main character in each story would do.

Larry's Story

Larry has just moved to town. He has not made new friends yet. Finally he is invited to a beach party that some of the kids in his class have been talking about. James, who is in his algebra class, offers to give him a ride to the beach. Larry is glad that he is beginning to fit in at his new school. He is enjoying the party very much. Then he realizes that James and several of the other kids have been pouring rum into their cola cans. He notices that

James is beginning to have a little trouble walking through the sand toward the parking lot. Larry . . .
- leaves James and goes home with other friends.
- joins James in drinking.
- asks James for the car keys so that he can drive James home.
- calls home to explain what has happened and asks for a ride home.

Jack's story

Everyone in Jack's group takes turns having a party. Jack is next. A lot of his friends drink. But his parents do not approve of kids drinking. Jack knows his parents will throw out anyone who sneaks alcohol into the party. Jack is caught between his parents' rules and what his friends expect for a good time. As the kids plan the upcoming party at Jack's house, Jack . . .
- tells them he's getting the flu.
- plans a trip out of town the night of the party.
- tries to think of ways to get his parents to change their minds.
- goes overboard with great food that he'll serve.
- tries to think of a plan for a theme and activities for the party. He hopes to get the kids' minds off the absence of alcohol.

For many people, social drinking means having one or two alcoholic drinks.

Chapter 3

Alcohol Users: Adults and Teenagers

any Americans drink alcohol. Most people drink it for pleasure and in small quantities. They do not depend on alcohol to get them through the day.

Adult Drinking

About 70 percent of adult Americans drink at least one alcoholic drink during a year.

Most people are social drinkers. Alcohol does not cause a problem for them. Social drinking is having a drink at a celebration. Or a drink before or after dinner. Or after a physical workout, such as playing in a sandlot baseball game.

Most social drinkers drink at home or at a party at someone else's home. People also drink socially in restaurants and bars. Some people have a drink when they travel on a train or a plane.

People Who Do Not Drink

About 30 percent of adult Americans in the United States do not drink alcoholic beverages. These people are called "abstainers" or "teetotalers."

Some people do not drink alcohol for religious reasons. Other reasons for not drinking include:

○ a dislike for the taste of alcohol.
○ the sick feeling some people get when they drink.
○ a dislike of drugs of any kind.
○ family members who have a problem with alcohol.

Drinking and Young People

Some teenagers experiment with alcohol to try out so-called adult behavior. They think drinking makes them "grown-up."

Adults become concerned about teenagers who do things that could be dangerous. Alcohol can turn into a problem for some teenagers. The most serious problem causes parents a great deal of concern.

In every state in the nation, teenagers cannot drink without breaking the law. Selling alcoholic beverages to people under the legal drinking age is a crime. Serving alcoholic beverages to that group is also a crime. Even parents who allow their children to serve alcoholic beverages at parties are breaking the law.

Being responsible about drinking is difficult. It involves judgment and maturity. It calls for an understanding of your own body and how it reacts to alcohol. And it requires the courage to be able to say no to something—even if all your friends are doing it. This is a big job. That is why state laws require kids to wait.

Health experts, too, have reason to be concerned. They have found that the younger a person starts drinking, the more likely it is that he or she will drink heavily as an adult.

According to recent surveys, young people today start drinking at an earlier age and more often than young people did in past years.

Beer and wine are usually the first drinks sampled by young people. Their first taste of alcohol may be a glass of wine at dinner. Or they may have wine at a religious service, or as a toast at a party.

Experts say that the reason for the trend toward early drinking is strong pressure from friends. A survey of more than 500,000 schoolchildren in the

United States shows the following facts about young people and alcohol:

○ About one third of all fourth graders (34 percent) report that they are pressured by kids their age to try beer, wine, or liquor.

○ Nine out of ten children in grades four, five, and six are aware that cocaine and marijuana are drugs. Less than five out of ten call alcohol a drug. Only one in five thinks of wine coolers as a drug. A *wine cooler* is a bottled mixture of wine and soda.

It can be hard for young people to say no to alcohol. But it is very important to be able to do it. Public health experts say that their studies show important things. Young people who drink alcohol regularly are taking real chances with their health. And they are taking risks with their future too. These young people often perform poorly in school. They become involved in crimes and accidents more often than others in their age group.

Teenage Drinking and Driving

An area of alcohol abuse that seriously affects teenagers is drunken driving. Pediatricians (doctors of children, preteens, and teenagers) report that the leading cause of death for young adults aged 15 to 24 years is driving under the influence of alcohol.

It is dangerous to drink and drive.

Experts say that young people tend to take more risks than adults when they get behind the wheel of a car. Risk-taking, inexperienced driving, and drinking can add up to serious trouble.

The Story of Sue and David

David adored his big sister, Sue. She taught him how to throw a ball. She helped make him the fastest swimmer on the school team.

Sue enjoyed being with David, too. She teased him a lot and called him her baby brother, but David knew they were pals.

Sue let David go along sometimes when she and her friends were out for a good time. One night a group of her teenage friends piled into Sue's wreck of a car. David tagged along. One of the guys went into a package store and bought a couple of six-packs of beer. David watched his sister guzzle two cans of beer and ask for a third. David had never seen his sister drink alcohol before.

Sue finished her third beer. Then she drove off to find another package store. She giggled a lot. She talked loudly. Some of her sentences didn't make much sense to David. She drove very fast.

Sue found a package store. Two of the kids went in. That's when Sue spotted David. He was huddled in the corner of the back seat, trying to be invisible.

Sue yelled at David. She said he should be home in bed. The other kids got back into the car. Sue revved the car out of the parking lot and tore off toward home.

At the corner of their street Sue slammed on the brakes. She yelled at David to get out of the car. David stood on the curb and watched the car roar away.

Sue was killed behind the wheel of the car soon after she took David home. The police blamed the accident on Sue—driving while intoxicated.

Chapter 4

The Effects of Alcohol on the Human Body

lcohol affects everyone who drinks it—men and women, old and young, experienced drinkers and people who drink for the first time.

Alcohol makes everyone who drinks it "feel different." One drink may make a person feel relaxed or happy. Or the person may simply feel different. A second drink may begin to slow the drinker down. More drinks may cause the drinker to fall asleep (pass out). A lot of liquor will result in a medical emergency for the drinker.

The reason a person is drinking also affects the drinker. Some reasons for drinking are appropriate. Others are not and may lead to problems.

The effects of alcohol differ from person to person. The effects may depend on the person's

31

body size. Generally, the larger the person, the more blood the person has to carry the alcohol around. A small teenager will feel the effect of alcohol more quickly and strongly than will a large adult. The teenager has less blood than the adult.

The type of drink being used also makes a difference. Alcoholic beverages contain different amounts of alcohol. A person who drinks four ounces of liquor takes in more alcohol than a person who drinks four ounces of beer.

The size of the drink is a factor. The more alcohol in a drink, the stronger the effects of that drink will be.

The length of time taken to drink makes a difference. An adult can probably handle four drinks over six hours. But if the adult has four drinks in *one* hour, he or she will most certainly feel the effects.

The amount of food in the stomach makes a difference, too. A person will get drunk more quickly on an empty stomach.

How a person is feeling when he or she drinks makes a difference. If a person drinks while tense, angry, uncomfortable, or tired from work, chances are that the effects of alcohol will be stronger. A problem is less likely if a person is comfortable and relaxed.

Another factor is "drug sensitivity." Some people are affected strongly by small amounts of alcohol, other drugs, and even medicines.

AREAS OF THE BODY AFFECTED BY ALCOHOL

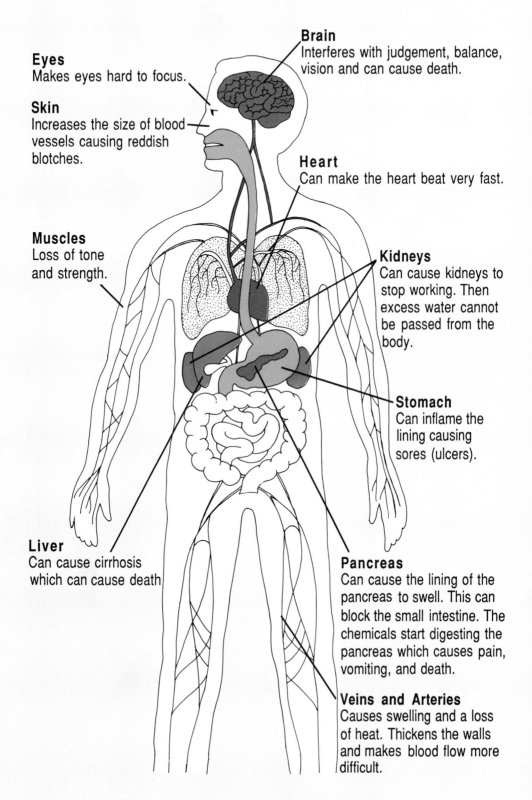

Eyes
Makes eyes hard to focus.

Skin
Increases the size of blood vessels causing reddish blotches.

Brain
Interferes with judgement, balance, vision and can cause death.

Heart
Can make the heart beat very fast.

Muscles
Loss of tone and strength.

Kidneys
Can cause kidneys to stop working. Then excess water cannot be passed from the body.

Stomach
Can inflame the lining causing sores (ulcers).

Liver
Can cause cirrhosis which can cause death

Pancreas
Can cause the lining of the pancreas to swell. This can block the small intestine. The chemicals start digesting the pancreas which causes pain, vomiting, and death.

Veins and Arteries
Causes swelling and a loss of heat. Thickens the walls and makes blood flow more difficult.

All of these factors affect how a person reacts, so it is easy to see how alcohol can affect people differently. Two people drinking the same drink can feel it differently. And the same drink on two occasions can affect the same person differently.

How Alcohol Affects the Body

Alcohol is a drug. It has a physical effect on every organ in the body from the moment it enters the system. Twenty percent of the alcohol taken into the body passes through the stomach into the bloodstream. It is carried in the bloodstream throughout the body.

The blood carries the alcohol to the brain. After one or two drinks, the drinker may feel warm and relaxed. After three or four drinks, speech becomes slurred and walking becomes difficult. The drinker has trouble focusing his eyes. After additional drinks, the drinker may not be able to talk or walk well at all.

If still more alcohol is put into the body, the drinker may pass out. The alcohol has depressed the workings of the brain.

The heavy drinker often feels the effects of alcohol the next morning. The drinker suffers a *hangover*. This means that he or she feels sick and may experience headache. The pounding headache is caused by overexpanded blood vessels in the brain.

A hangover lasts until the alcohol is completely out of the body. There is no fast cure for a hangover. Suggested cures such as black coffee, a cold shower, or physical workouts do not work. The only way to cure a hangover is to get sober. And that takes time.

The best way to avoid a hangover is not to drink alcohol.

How the Body Gets Rid of Alcohol

The body gets rid of alcohol in two ways: *elimination* and *oxidation*. Elimination gets rid of a small amount of the alcohol in the body; oxidation gets rid of most of it.

Elimination

The body eliminates most of the alcohol through the kidneys. The alcohol passes out of the body in urine.

A small amount of the alcohol is eliminated through the lungs. The blood carries the alcohol to the lungs, and there it is exhaled. A person who is drinking can have "whiskey breath." This is the result of alcohol evaporating when the person breathes out.

Perspiration also helps the body get rid of alcohol. Some alcohol leaves the body through the sweat glands.

Oxidation

Oxidation is the joining of a substance with oxygen. Through oxidation, the body burns off alcohol. In the body, alcohol is joined with carbon dioxide and water. Oxidation occurs mainly in the liver. But the liver can handle only a small amount of alcohol each hour. So most of the alcohol must stay in the bloodstream. It continues to flow to the organs, cells, and tissues of the body. It circulates until the liver can get rid of it. A person who drinks more alcohol in an hour than the liver can handle in that time will feel drunk.

Elimination and oxidation are the only ways the body can get rid of alcohol. Both processes take time.

How Alcohol Harms the Body

People who drink too much over a long period of time will find that alcohol can harm their health. This can happen even if they are not alcoholics. Three to four drinks a day on a regular basis can harm an adult body.

Large amounts of alcohol can harm the heart, veins, and arteries. Alcohol can thicken the walls of the arteries, raising the blood pressure. Alcohol causes the heart to beat faster, which can be dangerous for a person with heart disease.

Alcohol can cause kidney damage. If the kidneys fail, a person may die. A disease called *cirrhosis* of

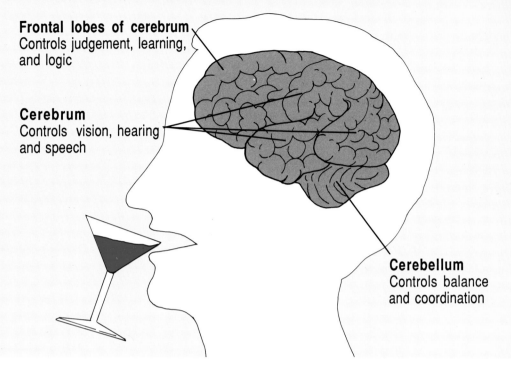

Frontal lobes of cerebrum
Controls judgement, learning, and logic

Cerebrum
Controls vision, hearing and speech

Cerebellum
Controls balance and coordination

the liver is often fatal. It strikes people who drink a lot of alcohol.

A woman who drinks at all during pregnancy passes the alcohol along to the fetus in her body. The alcohol affects the fetus, too. The fetus of a woman who drinks during pregnancy is at risk. The baby could be born deformed or with heart problems. Many children born to mothers who drink alcohol are born small. They may not grow normally. They may have learning problems later in life.

Alcohol abuse can injure the brain centers that control learning, judgment, and social actions. Large doses of alcohol can injure the parts of the brain that control breathing and heartbeat. Too much alcohol in the brain can cause death.

37

Alcohol can affect a heavy drinker in other ways, too. A person who is drunk can be aggressive, or tense, or depressed. These conditions can result in accidents, even suicide. They can destroy friendships and family life.

Alcohol use does not harm everyone's health. Most people can drink a small to moderate amount of alcohol on occasion. It will not cause them any harm.

But for some people, *any* amount of alcohol is harmful. These include people who have trouble with their heart, liver, stomach, or other organs. And there is another group of people who cannot drink alcohol at all. They have a disease. The disease is called alcoholism.

Too much alcohol can make a person aggressive.

Chapter 5

Alcoholism: What Is It?

Alcoholism is a disease. A person who suffers from alcoholism is called an alcoholic. Some alcoholics cannot get through a day without a drink. They let alcohol control their lives.

In the beginning the drinker can take alcohol or leave it alone. The drinker uses alcohol to have a good time. In time, however, the drinker misuses alcohol. He or she drinks to avoid facing problems.

Soon the drinker finds that alcohol begins to interfere with his or her life. The person has become a problem drinker. Problem drinkers can become *alcoholics*.

When Teens Drink

Drinking can cause many problems for teens. Drinking during school hours is a sure way to end up with poor grades. Students cannot concentrate if they have been drinking.

Drinking causes some teens to have run-ins with the law. They get into trouble because of vandalism or drunken driving.

Drinking can lead to alcoholism for teens too. Anyone can become an alcoholic.

Alcoholism and the Alcoholic

Health experts believe that problem drinking leads to alcoholism.

Alcoholism is a *chronic illness*. It is long-lasting. That means that alcoholics must stop drinking alcohol in order to be cured. And they can never drink again if they want to stay well.

Alcoholism creates problems for the drinker. It causes problems for the drinker's family, friends, coworkers, and neighbors. This disease has had a serious effect on many American lives.

Stages of Alcoholism

Alcoholism usually takes from five to seven years to develop. The disease is *progressive*. It develops in stages. The alcoholic goes through one stage at a time, over a long period of time. Most alcoholics

Taking a drink does not help anyone solve personal problems.

Stages of Alcoholism

First Stage (Warning Stage)

- Drinks too much to feel good.
- Drinks to get rid of stress.
- Goes from an occasional drink to daily drinks.
- Finds reasons to have a drink.
- Drinks more each time.
- Gets used to more alcohol in the body.

Second Stage (Danger Stage)

- Wants more alcohol.
- Becomes drunk more often.
- Blacks out occasionally, not remembering what happened.
- Drinks alone.
- Sneaks drinks.
- Gulps drinks.
- Feels guilty about drinking.
- Misses work (or school).

Third Stage (Losing Control Stage)

- Blames others for needing drink.
- Withdraws, rejects other people and shuts them out.
- Gets drunk often.
- Blacks out often.
- Spends money recklessly.
- Ignores responsibilities.
- Needs occasional hospitalization because of drinking.

Fourth Stage (Loss of Control Stage)

- Takes any kind of drug.
- Stops making excuses.
- Gets comfort from being drunk.
- Shakes.
- Fails at simple tasks.
- Faces death.

pass through all of the stages. Some alcoholics may not act in all the ways described in each stage. If the descriptions match the behavior of anyone you know, that person may be on the way to becoming an alcoholic. Or he or she may *be* an alcoholic. Do any of them describe you, or someone you know? You can get help. See Chapter 6.

Who Is an Alcoholic?

Anyone can be an alcoholic. It does not matter whether a person is rich or poor, an employed executive or an unemployed laborer, male or female, old or young. Alcoholism may be somewhat *hereditary* (passed on through the family). Studies show that more than half of today's alcoholics had at least one alcoholic parent, grandparent, or other close relative.

There are teenage alcoholics. Teens often start to drink alcohol early enough to be alcoholics by the time they reach high school.

Signs of Alcoholism

Signs of alcoholism are easy to spot during the time it takes for the disease to develop. The following questions highlight some of the early signs of alcoholism. They can help you find out if you or someone you know has a problem with alcohol.

o Do you drink alone?
o Do you sneak a drink in the morning?

Sneaking a drink may be an early sign of alcoholism.

○ Do you feel that you *need* a drink?
○ Do you ever become irritable when you drink?
○ Do you drink to get drunk?
○ Has your drinking harmed your family or friends in any way?
○ Does your drinking change your personality, creating a "new" you?
○ Are you more excited about doing things when you are drinking?
○ Do you drink to enjoy parties?
○ Does drinking make you moody?
○ Have you ever lost your memory (blacked out) when drinking?

If you, or someone you know, has a problem with alcohol, the next chapter will tell you how to get help.

Alcoholism: A Character Weakness or a Disease?

Authorities do not agree on what causes alcoholism. They realize that much research is needed. They are looking for solid answers to their questions about alcoholism.

For many years the drinker was blamed for alcoholism. People thought an alcoholic had a weak will, a poor character, or low values. Even today, some people argue that alcoholism is simply the result of "willful misconduct." They assert that an alcoholic can correct his behavior without help. They think that drinking or not drinking is a matter of discipline.

However, most health experts today call alcoholism a disease. This means that alcoholism, like most other illnesses, must be treated medically.

Calling alcoholism a sickness is a step forward. It means that alcoholics do not have to be ashamed of the problem. Nor do people who have an alcoholic parent, husband, or wife. They do not have to try to cover up the problem. Recognizing the disease and getting early treatment can make an important difference. Alcoholics can recover and return to a full life. But most alcoholics need help in order to recover. Both physical and emotional help are important. Support from family and friends can make a big difference. They can give a recovering alcoholic courage and hope.

Organizations like Alcoholics Anonymous can help people who have drinking problems.

Chapter 6

The Treatment of Alcoholism

The cost of alcohol abuse and alcoholism is huge. Lives are lost. Jobs are lost. Lives become disrupted, some forever. Billions of dollars are spent on medical treatments.

Without help, most alcoholics cannot stop drinking even if they want to. They crave alcohol. Their bodies have built up a need for it. They have to have a drink to get through the day. Life is very difficult for them without alcohol.

Help for Alcoholism

There are many kinds of treatment for alcoholics who want help. Alcoholics can get advice on where to go for treatment in their communities.

Many hospitals have clinics to help alcoholics.
Some special hospitals and homes treat only
alcoholics. Some treatment centers are residential.
The alcoholic must live there during the treatment.
But these are often very expensive. Other treatment
centers hold programs during the day or evening.
Patients can live at home and continue to work if
they are able.

What Is the Treatment for Alcoholism?

An alcoholic *can* stop drinking. But the alcoholic
must have treatment. Each patient must find a
treatment that works for him or her. Doctors,
priests or ministers, and health and social workers
can help alcoholics decide what kind of treatment
will be best for them.

Detoxification is an important step in the
treatment of alcoholism. This process gets rid of
all alcohol in the body. After detoxification the
physical need for alcohol is gone, as long as the
person doesn't drink again.

Detoxification is usually done in a hospital.
This is because a person can suffer tremors,
hallucinations, and mental stress during withdrawal
from alcohol.

Even after detoxification, it is very hard for an
alcoholic to stay away from alcohol. Most treatment
centers tell their patients never to have another
alcoholic drink. The only way for them to live well

and stay healthy is to avoid alcohol completely. One drink, and its effect on the body, can mean the return of the person's dependence on alcohol.

Treatment centers teach the alcoholic how to live without alcohol. They can help "problem drinkers" too. These are people who are not physically dependent on alcohol, but who drink a lot and drink often. The problem drinker learns that he or she *can* handle problems, have fun, be social, relax, make friends, and feel good about himself or herself *without* alcohol.

Alcoholics Anonymous

This famous self-help organization for alcoholics was founded in 1935 by two alcoholics. They helped each other when they couldn't get help anywhere else. They started Alcoholics Anonymous by talking each other into staying sober one day at a time. Alcoholics Anonymous, called AA for short, helps people who want to stop drinking. It helps them stay away from alcohol.

AA members meet in groups. Members admit their problems to each other and talk about their experiences with alcoholism. In return, the group gives them understanding and support.

There are about 34,000 AA groups in the United States. If you think joining AA could help someone you know, tell him or her about it. The phone number of the group nearest you is listed in the telephone book.

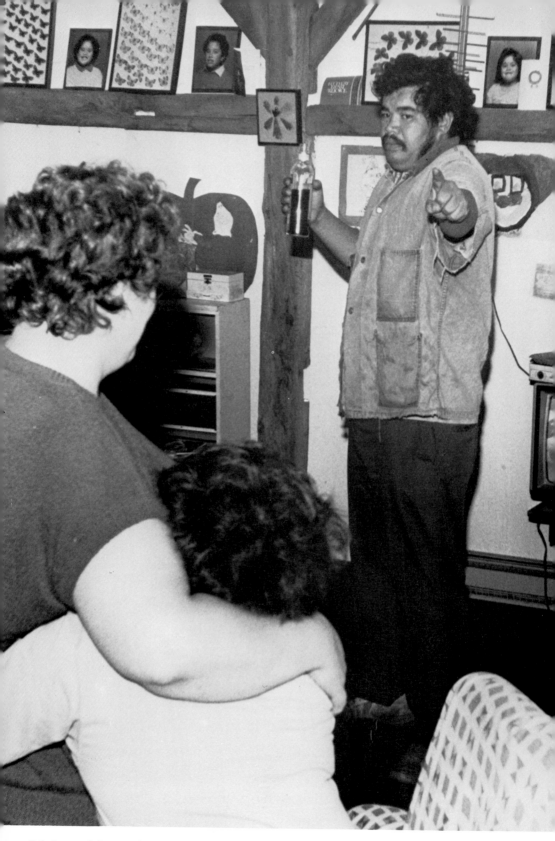

Living with an alcoholic affects the whole family.

Chapter 7

Alcohol and You

Studies show that more and more adults are drinking less and less. However, drinking attracts many young people.

The facts about young drinkers are not good. One out of fifteen teens who are attracted by alcohol will become an alcoholic. One out of four teenage drinkers will get into trouble as a result of drinking.

Alcoholism Affects Nondrinkers, Too

Some of you who do not drink have a problem with alcohol nevertheless. Many of you are living with a parent or another member of your family who is addicted to alcohol. In the United States, 18 million adults are problem drinkers. One family in four has been troubled by alcohol.

Alcohol Affects Family Life

Alcoholism is often a family illness. Every person in the family is affected. Often a family has problems before a family member becomes an alcoholic. Here are some of the problems an alcoholic's family must cope with:

○ An alcoholic can be happy one minute and angry the next, talkative one minute, then silent.
○ An alcoholic often neglects work, health, housekeeping, and friendships. If work is neglected, the family may have money problems.
○ An alcoholic who tries to cover up a drinking problem can become withdrawn and unfriendly.

Sometimes family members help cover up the problem. They avoid friends and social events. They are afraid of questions about the alcoholic in the family. Children stop bringing friends home. The situation is very stressful (difficult) for everyone.

Members of an alcoholic's family often feel guilty. Sometimes they feel the problem is their fault. They feel they should be able to help solve the problem. They wish family life could go back to what it was before alcohol entered their lives.

The guilt grows when they realize that they resent having to live with a problem drinker or an alcoholic.

If someone in your family is an alcoholic, try to be supportive and helpful. But you should not feel guilty if you cannot help someone you love to recover from alcoholism. It is a disease. And it is that person's problem—a problem only he or she can solve.

Alcoholism in the Family: The Story of Carley

Carley was in a good mood when she got off the school bus. The drama teacher had asked her to try out for a part she wanted in the school play.

But as Carley reached her street, her mood darkened. She felt her stomach muscles tighten. From the outside, her house looked fine. But inside was another story. Carley never knew from day to day what her mother would be like when she got home.

"Why are you so late!" her mother screamed from the living room when Carley stepped inside.

It took Carley some time to spot her mother in the dark living room. She was sitting in the corner, still in her bathrobe. She was holding a glass and the remote control for the TV.

"I've been waiting for you to fix this control. It doesn't work! It never did." She flung the control across the room. "And dinner," she yelled. "It should have been started an hour ago."

"I'll get to it. But first I'll fix the TV for you." Carley picked up the remote control. Then she turned on the TV. Her mother had not done that.

Carley ran out of the room. She didn't want to say something she would regret. How could she ever bring a date into the house? How could she stand the embarrassment of someone meeting her mother? How could she find time for play rehearsals? Her mother needed her.

At school the next day Carley went to rehearsal. But she wondered why she bothered. "You're one

A child may feel responsible for an alcoholic parent.

of the best students I've had," Mr. Burke told Carley. "You really are talented." Carley started to cry. "I don't think I can be in the play," she stammered. Then she ran out of the classroom.

That night Carley sat alone at the table, eating a roll and a cup of canned soup. She wished she could talk to her mother about what had happened. But earlier her mother had stumbled up the stairs to pass out on her bed.

The doorbell rang. Carley froze. Would her mother wake up and want to come downstairs? Carley ran to get the door before a second ring. Mr. Burke was at the door.

"May I come in?" he asked. Carley stared. "Yes, come in," Carley managed to say, remembering her manners.

"Where's your mom?" he asked.

"Ah, she . . . she's in bed. She went up early," Carley stumbled.

"Nothing serious, I hope?" Mr. Burke asked. "I thought the three of us could pick up where we left off when you ran out this afternoon. You see, I don't believe you want to drop out of the play."

"I *do*," Carley blurted out angrily. "And Mom doesn't want to talk to you about me. She doesn't care about me or about anything these days."

There was a long pause. Then Mr. Burke asked, "Does she drink?"

"Mom? Drink? Yes, a little," Carley said softly, surprised at her honesty. She stared at the floor.

"She started drinking when Dad died. I guess raising me alone was tough. Lonely. I tried, but I couldn't take his place."

"Her drinking has nothing to do with you or your dad, Carley. I knew your mom when your dad was living. Even then I thought she had a disease. It's called alcoholism. She needs help."

"You mean a doctor?" Carley asked. "In a hospital?"

"For sure a doctor, and maybe a hospital," Mr. Burke said. "I can help you talk to her. As for you, you need help, too. You can go with my son Mark to his next meeting. He belongs to a special support group for children of alcoholics. There are a lot of kids your age in the group. They'll help you understand the problems you have living with an alcoholic. You can solve the problems, you know. Then next year, you'll be doing what you want to do, I'm sure of it."

"Did you say I could go with Mark, your son?"

"Yes. Not many people know it, but Mark has parents who are recovering alcoholics, my wife and I. Mark has found out that drinkers can get help."

Help for the Family of an Alcoholic

If you live with an alcoholic, you should know that you are not alone with your problems. Many people live with people who are problem drinkers.

Fortunately, help is available for these people. Two of the help groups have grown out of

Support groups can help people who live with alcoholics.

Alcoholics Anonymous. One is *Al-Anon,* a support group for the family. Another is *Alateen,* a support group for children of alcoholics.

Al-Anon helps the wives and husbands of alcoholics. Al-Anon meetings help members deal with the alcoholic's problems and their own problems.

Alateen helps young people understand their parent's problems and the disease of alcoholism.

Alcoholics Anonymous, Al-Anon, and Alateen keep their memberships and attendance at meetings private. This means that people can seek help without being embarrassed.

Family Support

The reaction of the alcoholic's family to the problems caused by alcohol affects the alcoholic.

57

Support of family members is important to treatment of an alcoholic and his or her recovery. An alcoholic needs help and support to deal with the disease.

Here are some ways members of an alcoholic's family can cope with the problems brought on by alcohol:

○ Learn as much as you can about alcohol and its use.

○ Learn as much as you can about the disease of alcoholism.

○ Think about how you feel about alcoholism.

○ Try to understand how the alcoholic you know is affecting your life.

○ Attend Al-Anon or Alateen meetings to learn from the experiences of others.

○ Discuss your problems with someone you trust— a counselor, a doctor, a priest, a rabbi, or a minister.

○ Remember that you are not the cause of the problem.

○ Remember that alcoholism is a disease from which a person can recover.

Are You in the Know?

We hope that after you have read this book you have a better understanding of what drinking alcohol is all about.

The next time someone offers you a drink, try to remember what you have learned.

Glossary—*Explaining New Words*

abstinence Not doing something.

abuse To use a thing wrongly.

addict One who is dependent upon alcohol or another drug.

Al-Anon Group of wives and husbands of alcoholics who meet to discuss alcoholism and how to help their alcoholic spouses.

Alateen Group of teenage children of alcoholics who meet to learn about the disease of alcoholism and about how to help themselves and their families.

alcoholic Person suffering from the disease of alcoholism.

alcoholic beverage Any drink that is at least 2 percent alcohol.

Alcoholics Anonymous Worldwide nonprofit organization that helps people who want to stop drinking alcoholic beverages.

alcoholism Disease in which the body depends on alcohol and the drinker loses control when alcohol is used.

blackout Period of time when a drinker cannot remember what happened during or after drinking alcohol.

cirrhosis Disease, often associated with alcoholism, in which the liver and sometimes the kidneys become scarred and hardened.

depressant Drug that slows down the body.

detoxification. Treatment for alcoholism in which the patient's body is made free of alcohol.

drug Substance that affects the human body. Most drugs are intended to treat disease

drunkenness State of temporary partial loss of control over the body and its reactions because too much alcohol is taken in.

DWI Drinking while intoxicated; drunken driving.

fetus Unborn child.

hereditary characteristic Characteristic that runs in a family.

intoxication Drunkenness.

kidneys Two bean-shaped organs that take in liquid waste from the body and pass it out in urine.

liquor Distilled alcohol such as rye, bourbon, or scotch whiskey.

liver Large organ in the body that helps digest food.

oxidation The joining of a substance with oxygen.

problem drinker A person who misuses alcohol.

prohibition A law of the United States from 1920 to 1933 that made illegal the sale, manufacture, and transportation of alcoholic beverages.

reflexes Involuntary movements of the body; movements that occur without thought or effort, such as when a finger touches a hot stove.

sober Not under the influence of alcohol.

social drinker A person who drinks alcohol with other people as an act of friendship or to be social.

Where To Go for Help

Alcoholics Anonymous (AA)
National Headquarters
P.O. Box 459, Grand Central Station
New York, New York 19163
(212) 686-1100

Al-Anon Family Group Headquarters, Inc.
P.O. Box 182, Madison Square Station
New York, New York 10159
1-800-356-9996
(212) 245-3151 (from New York and Canada)

Alateen
P.O. Box 182, Madison Square Garden
New York, New York 10159

National Association for Children of Alcoholics
31706 Coast Highway, Suite 201
South Laguna, California 92677
(714) 499-3889

Students To Offset Peer Pressure (STOPP)
P.O. Box 103, Department S
Hudson, New Hampshire 03051-0103

For Help With Drunk Driving Problems

AAA Foundation for Traffic Safety
2990 Telestar Court, Suite 100
Falls Church, Virginia 22042

SADD (Students Against Driving Drunk)
Box 800
Marlboro, Massachusetts 01752

MADD (Mothers Against Drunk Driving)
669 Airport Freeway, Suite 310
Hurst, Texas 76053

For Further Reading

Bregman, M. "I'm Keith, and I'm an Alcoholic." *Choices*, December 1986, pages 14–15 +. This article tells one young person's story about alcohol abuse and recovery.

Englebardt, S. L. "When Your Child Drinks." *Reader's Digest*, November 1986, pages 110–114. This article discusses the symptoms and the problems related to alcohol abuse by young people.

"How Alcoholics Anonymous Works." *Choices*, December 1986, page 17. This article is about the most famous alcoholism treatment organization, and the way its program is conducted.

Hyde, Margaret O. *Know About Alcohol*. New York: McGraw-Hill, 1978, 80 pages. This book is about drinking and how to deal with social situations (parties, etc.) where alcohol is involved.

Lee, Essie E. and Elaine Israel. *Alcohol and You*. New York: Messner, 1975, 64 pages. This book tells the history of alcohol use. It deals with the effects of alcohol on the body and with the problems alcohol use can cause for young people.

Leite, Evelyn and Pamela Espeland. *Different Like Me* Minneapolis: Johnson Institute Books, 1987, 110 pages. This book is for teens who have parents with alcohol problems.

Salk, L. "Children and Drinking: What Parents Can Do." *McCalls*, June 1985, page 58. This article discusses ways parents can help their children avoid problems with alcohol.

Seixas, Judith S. *Alcohol: What it Does*. New York: Greenwillow Books, 1977, 56 pages. This book is about the ways that alcohol affects your body and your mind.

Index

About the Author
Barbara Taylor is a writer/editor at Weekly Reader in Middletown,
Connecticut. She has taught in Japan, France, and Germany as well
as in elementary classrooms in Massachusetts.

About the Editor
Evan Stark is a well-known sociologist, educator, and therapist
as well as a popular lecturer on women's and children's health issues.
Dr. Stark was the Henry Rutgers Fellow at Rutgers University, an as-
sociate at the Institution for Social and Policy Studies at Yale University, and a Fulbright Fellow at the University of Essex. He is the author
of many publications in the field of family relations and is the father of
four children.

Acknowledgments and Photo Credits

P. 11, 12, 33, 37 Sonja Kalter; all other photos, Stuart Rabinowitz

Design/Production: Blackbirch Graphics, Inc.
Cover Photograph: Stuart Rabinowitz

DATE DUE

FE 19 '92	NV 20 79		
MR 17 '92			
AP 29 '92			
SE 25 '93			
JN 17 95			
MY 03 '00			
NO 08 '00			
MO 21 10			
AG 18 10			
NO 3 10			

DEMCO